MW01234657

Heaven

YOUR AMAZING JOURNEY HOME

Randy Lariscy

WordTruth Press
USA

1st Edition
Published by WordTruth Press
(SAN 920-2811)
Marietta, Georgia (USA)
Website: WordTruthPress.com
eMail: Info@WordTruthPress.com

ISBN: 978-1-944758-00-4

Library of Congress Control Number: 2015960984

Additional books by Randy Lariscy

Natural Evangelism

Portraits of Forgiveness

Speedy Devotions (Vol. 1) – Wise Choices

The Book of Mark (Vol. 1)

Acknowledgements

To all the people in my life - my family, friends, neighbors, coworkers, tennis buddies, servers, cashiers, and the multitude of random people I encounter every day - this book is for you. I love people, period. And I want to see you make it to your home in Heaven someday as part of God's family. Then we will all be family. What a great day that will be!

Contents

Introduction

The word *home* evokes strong memories for most people. For some the memories are mostly wonderful but for others home connotes a very sordid life best forgotten. An abusive father or absentee mother makes home a place to avoid. But no matter your upbringing, the LORD has something absolutely outstanding planned for you. Your future home, your real home - the one God has in mind for you - is a place called Heaven.

Do you see Heaven as a place to look forward to one day or is it something mystical, perhaps even mythical for you? Have you any certainty about what will happen to you when you pass from this life?

HEAVEN

Can you believe the amazing stories that people with near-death experiences (NDE) tell us about what Heaven is like? These and many more questions about Heaven are discussed in this book.

What we know for certain about Heaven can only be addressed accurately by one person - the One who created Heaven. In the Bible, the LORD Jesus gave us this preface about Heaven:

> *My Father's house has many rooms; if that were not so, would I have told you that I am going there to prepare a place for you? And if I go and prepare a place for you, I will come back and take you to be with me that you also may be where I am. (John 14:2-3, NIV®)*

Heaven is truly an amazing place and Jesus tells us that it is a place for you. So sit down, relax, put your feet up, and read about this amazing future home. When you finish this book and understand the reality of Heaven, *home* will forevermore be a word that evokes hope and joy. Heaven can be your certain future. See you on the other side!

For His kingdom,

Randy Lariscy
(Acts 20:24)

If This is Heaven...

In children's cartoons, you inevitably see a person who dies and, presumably, goes to Heaven. The person appears ghostlike with angel's wings and a harp to play. Heaven is portrayed as a cloud where you sit and strum a harp forever.

Boring!

HEAVEN

If Heaven is anything like this, I do not want to go there and I'm sure you feel the same way. There are many other misconceptions about Heaven:

- **Myth** - it does not exist at all. When you die, you cease to exist totally. There is no afterlife.

- **Choir practice** - you sit around all day, every day, in a perpetual worship service.

- **Your favorite thing to do** - Heaven is fishing, shopping, eating or whatever your most favorite thing in the world happens to be.

- **Family and Friends** - A fun place where all the people you know and love will be with you.

It is a bit difficult to wrap your head around the concept of Heaven. We live in a tangible world with a physical body. The idea of existence beyond our present existence is hard to comprehend. Perhaps this is why there are so many different ideas about the afterlife.

Near-death experiences (NDE) offer interesting insights into what Heaven might be like. Many NDE's describe a bright light, a tunnel, a beautiful place of great peace and joy, with many loved ones who had gone on before. While there are many similarities in NDE accounts, there are differences as well. And many who have attested to a NDE *(making money from books and movies that tell their story)* have later recanted. So how can you believe someone who shares an amazing NDE?

The truth is you cannot deny someone had an experience. I tend to assume someone is telling me the truth until I find out otherwise. Since there is no way to affirm or disprove someone's experience, I usually smile and listen but never argue with them. What good would it do anyway? It was their experience, not mine.

What we can do is try to understand if the *Heaven* they saw in their NDE was anything like the real deal. The real *Heaven* is not one we discern from someone's story but from the One who actually created Heaven. Only someone that we know has been there can accurately describe Heaven. And that someone is the LORD Jesus. The Bible tells us that Jesus:

Created Heaven	Through him all things were made; without him nothing was made that has been made. (John 1:3, NIV®)
Came From Heaven	What does "he ascended" mean except that he [Jesus] also descended to the lower, earthly regions? He who descended is the very one who ascended higher than all the heavens, in order to fill the whole universe. (Ephesians 4:9-10, NIV®)
Arranges Heaven	[Jesus said]: I am going there to prepare a place for you. (John 14:2, NIV®)
Takes People to Heaven	[Jesus prayed]: Father, I want those you have given me to be with me where I am, and to see my glory, the glory you have given me because you loved me before the creation of the world. (John 17:24, NIV®)

Jesus alone has the authority to explain Heaven to us. Only He can accurately describe what Heaven is like (and show us how to get there - more on that later). What you will find is that Heaven is such an amazing place, you will want make your home there someday. The good news is that Jesus wants you to come home someday and be with Him in Heaven. So keep reading and find out next about His heavenly promise.

The Promise of a Home Just For You

If I imagined the perfect place for me it would be on the beach. I love watching the sunset on beautiful beaches. The perfect beach would have some people but definitely room for me - and my umbrella and cooler with goodies to snack on and a good book to read and ... well, you get the picture.

What's the perfect place for your home? Maybe you like the mountains or the place where you currently live is just fine. No matter what your ideal place might be, Jesus is preparing an absolutely perfect home just for you. In fact, He promised:

> *My Father's house has many rooms; if that were not so, would I have told you that I am going there to prepare a place for you? And if I go and prepare a place for you, I will come back and take you to be with me that you also may be where I am. (John 14:2-3, NIV®)*

Jesus is preparing a beautiful place called Heaven with many rooms - translated *"mansions"* in the some Bible versions. In describing God and heavenly things, the

Bible often uses human terms to help us better understand. Will they actually be elegant mansions, gleaming white rooms, or something else? Only Jesus knows.

The point Jesus is making here is that there is ample room and He has a specific home for you. Heaven is that place where you will live forever after this earthly life has ended. Jesus gives you this assurance of His word: *"If it were not so, I would have told you."* (v2)

Heaven is also the place where you will live with Jesus forever: *"I will come back and take you to be with me that you also may be where I am."* (v3) Now some people make promises they intend to keep but, somehow, never get around to it. Others make promises just to make you feel good (or feel better when things are not going your way).

Perhaps you had a mother or father who made many promises they never kept. It is hard to trust anyone when the people closest to you break their promises, is it not?

Not so with Jesus. You can trust His words. Both friends and enemies confirmed that He spoke the truth. Jesus performed many miracles specifically to point to the truth of what He was teaching. And He made some amazing predictions about His life and every one of those predictions came true. You can read more about this in the appendix: *You Can Trust What Jesus Says*.

So when Jesus made this promise of a perfect home, you can trust Him implicitly. And never forget the most important part of what He promised - *"for you."* (vv. 2-3) Jesus specifically wants *you* to make *your* home

with Him forever in the perfect place called
Heaven.

Are you ready to find out what Heaven will
really be like? No travel brochure on Earth
could do justice to the beauty and wonder of
Heaven. So next let's take a look at how
Jesus described Heaven.

A Hometown You Have to See

Have you ever been on a trip to a new place
and saw incredible sights you have never
seen before? *Hey, we don't have that in my
hometown.* Thinking of that kind of thrill,
multiply the feeling by *billions* and you will
have but a glimpse at what is in store for
you in Heaven. In a very practical way,

talking about the wonder and beauty of Heaven is an attempt to describe the indescribable.

Yet we do have some insights into Heaven. Jesus revealed much about Heaven to His apostle John. Here is a snippet of his description of Heaven's beauty:

The wall was made of jasper, and the city of pure gold, as pure as glass. The foundations of the city walls were decorated with every kind of precious stone. The first foundation was jasper, the second sapphire, the third agate, the fourth emerald, the fifth onyx, the sixth ruby, the seventh chrysolite, the eighth beryl, the ninth topaz, the tenth turquoise, the eleventh jacinth, and the twelfth amethyst. The twelve gates were twelve pearls, each gate made of a single pearl. The great street of the city was of gold, as pure as transparent glass. (Revelation 21:18-21, NIV®)

From an earthly point of view, Heaven is seen as a place of unimaginable beauty:

♦ A city of totally pure gold - 24K gold

♦ Walls composed of every kind of precious gem and stone

♦ Huge gates each made of a single pearl

♦ Even the streets are paved with pure gold

Consider the story of a smart businessman who died in a sudden accident:

Before the angel could take him to Heaven, the businessman negotiated to bring whatever he wanted in one suitcase. The angel was puzzled at why he wanted to bring anything with him but helped him anyway on his journey to the pearly gates.

St. Peter welcomed him to Heaven. Then he saw the suitcase and asked what he brought with him. The man opened his briefcase showing it was full of gold bullion. With a slight smirk, St. Peter asked, "You brought pavement?" [i]

Earthly riches simply cannot compare to what awaits in Heaven. The description using gems, precious stones, and gold points to the limitless beauty and value of the home Jesus is preparing for you in Heaven. Your life on Earth may be devoid of wealth and tragic circumstances may rob your joy, blinding you to anything beautiful. Rest assured that in Heaven your circumstances will be dramatically different, better, and secure.

Also consider how you view your earthly possessions in light of the beauty and wonder of Heaven. What you have today is nothing compared to what God has in store for you in eternity. Your cars, homes, paintings, bank account - none of it will last here on Earth. Yet heavenly things will never wear out. God's rewards in Heaven are eternal.

So take the advice of Corrie Ten Boom - a remarkable Christian woman who, during

World War II, helped scores of Jews by hiding them in a secret room built in her home. She eventually was discovered and her whole family was sent to prison. After the war, Corrie set up a camp for the holocaust survivors. She captured her experiences in the book, *The Hiding Place*. One of the conclusions Corrie had about life is to *"Hold everything in your hands lightly, otherwise it hurts when God pries your fingers open."* [ii]

Heaven is a place of such wonder and beauty that it can never be adequately described in human words. You will just have to see it for yourself. And who else will be there to visit your new home in Heaven? Turn the page and have a look at your companions on this heavenly journey.

[i] *Source unknown though this story in various forms is found unattributed on many websites.*
[ii] Boom, Corrie Ten. Retrieved 1/31/2016 at https://twitter.com/CorrieTenBoom/status/2552260091.

Home For All Sorts of People

I must admit that I am not a *big event* kind of person. Some people love being part of a huge crowd like the excited fans at this football game. It makes me kind of nervous - but that's just me. One thing you do find at big events is not just a large crowd of people but a great diversity of people. You find people from all walks of life, different countries, men, women, boys, girls, rich, poor, happy, sad, and everything in-between.

Heaven is also going to have people - a lot of people - from many different walks of life. Good news for you because God has no limit on the number of tickets to Heaven:

> *After this I looked, and there before me was a great multitude that no one could count, from every nation, tribe, people and language, standing before the throne and before the Lamb. They were wearing white robes and were holding palm branches in their hands. And they cried out in a loud voice: "Salvation belongs to our God, who sits on the throne, and to the Lamb." (Revelation 7:9-10, NIV®)*

Does your current home have this diversity of people? Heaven will include a *"great multitude"* of people from *"every nation."* (v. 9) Currently the Earth holds nearly 300 nations or national entities[iii] each with their own culture and language. Even within these nations, you can find different people groups, cultures, and families with multiple languages spoken. It is a world divided into many unique slices of people groups.

Yet in Heaven, there is no racial exclusion, no economic exclusion, and no nationalities excluded. A great diversity of people will be in unity. All will be gathered together in one place, everyone wearing the same thing, with a common faith in God. We will even worship the LORD Jesus[iv] with one voice. You see, in Heaven we will have a common language, just as it was in the beginning when God created humans to roam and rule the Earth.[v]

HEAVEN

It would take a miracle, you say. Diverse groups do not generally join together in harmony. And you would be right. Heaven is nothing if not miraculous.

While we strive today for *peace on Earth and good will to all people*, we constantly fall short. Why can't we all be friends here on Earth? Why can't we all get along?

Some say, *if they had a common faith, different groups of people could get along, right?* Yet we see division and segregation among churches, even in the same denomination. Or *if they all spoke the same language, different groups would get along better, right?* Sadly we know this does not solve the problem either. Perfect people could get along just fine - but there are no perfect people on Earth.

Let us be honest here. Each of us has an innate quality of self-concern - at least that is the positive spin we like to think about ourselves. I*t is just part of my survival instinct, right?* But when we look closely in the mirror, we see that self-concern too often deteriorates into self-centeredness, selfishness, and an attitude of self-determination creating all manner of conflict and division in our lives. Family relationships are broken, communities squabble, and fighting occurs all over the globe. Try as we may, no human has ever found a way to rid that innate quality that divides us as a people.

In His description of Heaven we saw earlier, Jesus noted the people there will wear *"white robes"* (v. 10), a symbol of their purity and righteousness. Heaven is not a place for perfect people but for *perfected* people. God in His great love and mercy makes it possible for you to be perfected. And He desires to perfect you, wanting *"... All people to be saved."* (1 Timothy 2:4, NIV®)

Do you know the way to this extravagant home God is preparing to house you along with so many others from all over the world? Jesus told His disciples:

> *"You know the way to the place where I am going. Thomas said to him, "Lord, we don't know where you are going, so how can we know the way?" Jesus answered, "I am the way and the truth and the life. No one comes to the Father except through me. " (John 14:4-6, NIV®)*

While some may question Jesus' claim to be the only way to Heaven, I thank God that there is a way at all - for I surely do not deserve it. Do you?

What a great comfort to know that God has provided a way that enables human beings to be perfected so they can live together in harmony in our future home called Heaven. There will be neither division nor segregation nor enemies in Heaven. God's plan is to remove that innate quality of self-centeredness and replace it with love and righteousness instead.   He took it upon Himself to do *for* us what we could not do *by* ourselves.

Next we will see how Heaven will satisfy our deepest longing for love - someone for you to love and be loved in return.

---

iii CIA.gov. The World Factbook. Retrieved 2/10/2016 at https://www.cia.gov/library/publications/the-world-factbook/.

iv The reference to the "Lamb" in Revelation 7:9-10 is to Jesus Christ. The prophet, John the Baptist, referred to Jesus as "the Lamb of God, who takes away the sin of the world!" (John 1:29, NIV®)

v Now the whole world had one language and a common speech. (Genesis 11:1, NIV®)

Where Everybody Knows Your Name

A popular TV show back in the 1980's was set in a local pub with an eclectic group of people who shared one thing in common - their home away from home which was the pub named *Cheers*. The tagline of the show revealed the depth of that common bond. It was the place where *"everybody knows your name."*

Wouldn't it be great to be in a place where everyone not only accepted you but deeply loved you?

HEAVEN

My wife and I got to know a very dear older gentleman named Bobby. He was one of the most encouraging souls I have ever met. The moment you entered Bobby's presence, you felt like you were the most important person around. He would give my wife a big hug and say, "You know you are my favorite!" My wife would just melt at those words.

One evening we were at a gathering and saw Bobby across the room talking to a group of ladies. My wife made a beeline over to Bobby to get her hug. As she walked up, she heard Bobby say to one of the ladies, "You know you are my favorite!" My wife tapped him on the shoulder and sternly said, "You said I was your favorite." Bobby blushed a little and with a big grin said, "You are my favorite. You are all my favorites!"

Heaven is going to be a place where you are everyone's favorite. On Earth, we struggle to truly love even one person deeply, much less a crowd of people. In Heaven, your capacity to love people is going to be so enlarged that you will be able to say in truth, *"You are all my favorites!"*

Jesus prayed this future for all who would believe in Him:

> *I in them and you in me—so that they may be brought to complete unity. Then the world will know that you sent me and* <u>*have loved them even as you have loved me*</u>. *Father, I want those you have given me to be with me where I am [in Heaven], and to see my glory, the glory you have given me because you loved me before the creation of the world. Righteous Father, though the world does not know you, I know you, and they know that you have sent me. I have made you known to them, and will continue to make you known* <u>*in order that the love you have for me may be in them*</u> *and that I myself may be in them. (John 17:23-26, NIV®)*

Jesus wants you experience the love He knows - the kind of love that God the Father has for His only Son. And Jesus demonstrated His love for you when He gave His life on a cross to pay the penalty for your sins: *"While we were still sinners, Christ died for us."* (Romans 5:8, NIV®)

Your own capacity to love others is fueled by how much you are loved. Incredible as it seems, the amazing love that Jesus has for you is the love He desires to implant in your soul so that Heaven will be a place where you and everyone else is welcomed and completely loved.

Think about how your life would change if, today, you were deeply and completed loved by someone who would, without question or hesitation, give his life for you. What would be your level of:

- ♦ Joy?

- ♦ Companionship?

- ♦ Security?

- ♦ Hope?

- ♦ Satisfaction?

In this present world we cannot experience this kind of love from everyone, nor can we love others perfectly. What we can experience is the complete and perfect love of just One - the LORD Jesus. Entering into a relationship of love with Him gives you a glimpse into the perfect love you can look forward to in Heaven. Trusting in Him by faith gives you certain hope in your future home where *everybody knows your name.*

Next find out how the newness of Heaven shines its special light on your everyday pains and problems.

A New and Better Home

When I was growing up, we moved every few years. On the one hand, I had to leave behind my friends. But I was able to move into a new house, new neighborhood, new friends, and new adventures. The new house itself was better than the old house - usually bigger, all new and clean, and all the appliances and devices worked.

Heaven will be a new home for you, a much better home:

HEAVEN

God's dwelling place is now among the people, and he will dwell with them. They will be his people, and God himself will be with them and be their God. 'He will wipe every tear from their eyes. There will be no more death' or mourning or crying or pain, for the old order of things has passed away." He who was seated on the throne said, "I am making everything new!" (Revelation 21:3-5, NIV®)

Back on Earth, loneliness is a universal complaint as explained by Japanese writer Haruki Murakami:

Why do people have to be this lonely? What's the point of it all? Millions of people in this world, all of them yearning, looking to others to satisfy them, yet isolating themselves. Why? Was the earth put here just to nourish human loneliness? [vi]

When you look at the world as it exists today, it does make you wonder why God would have created it this way. The old order of things is how the world currently operates. Death is an ugly part of our lives. Pain, tears, and loss are inevitable in a world of people with a self-focused attitude.

It was not this way in the beginning as God originally designed things. Thankfully, it will not be this way in the end. In Heaven, God will dwell with us and among us. Loneliness will be extinct and forgotten as God and all His people will be gathered together in this new and better home.

Loneliness will not be the only travail we leave behind. There will be no death in Heaven, no tears, no pain, no mourning of loss. All of these tragedies are part of the old order of things. Heaven is a new, different, and eternally better home.

HEAVEN

The city was laid out like a square, as long as it was wide. He measured the city with the rod and found it to be 12,000 stadia in length, and as wide and high as it is long. The angel measured the wall using human measurement, and it was 144 cubits thick ... The city does not need the sun or the moon to shine on it, for the glory of God gives it light, and the Lamb is its lamp. The nations will walk by its light, and the kings of the earth will bring their splendor into it. On no day will its gates ever be shut, for there will be no night there. (Revelation 21:16-17, 23-25 NIV®)

Consider this heavenly city where we will live:

♦ **As is said today, "It's Yuuuge!"** - the city will be 12,000 stadia (roughly 1,400 miles) wide, long, and high. One city in the form of a cube that is about a third the size of the Earth.

♦ **Security is not an issue** - the walls are 144 cubits thick (roughly 200 feet). This city is not going anywhere. Your home there will be safe.

♦ **Come and go as you please** - the large, magnificent gates forged out of single pearls will never be shut. There is no night in Heaven and no bandits at night to plunder and pillage.

♦ **No electric bill** - God Himself, full of glory, will literally light up Heaven forever.

Hey, what about food? I know there are quite a few dishes I consider heavenly.

Then the angel showed me the river of the water of life, as clear as crystal, flowing from the throne of God and of the Lamb 2 down the middle of the great street of the city. On each side of the river stood the tree of life, bearing twelve crops of fruit, yielding its fruit every month. And the leaves of the tree are for the healing of the nations. 3 No longer will there be any curse. (Revelation 22:1-3, NIV®)

God provides heavenly food from the tree of life, unique in two respects. First, it bears fruit every month of every year (these are human terms used to describe heavenly things). Second, it brings health and well-being to all who partake.

Back in the beginning, we saw this tree of life on Earth in the Garden of Eden. After the first man (Adam) and first woman (Eve) sinned against the LORD's command, they were banished from the garden specifically to keep them from eating from the tree of life. While this seems unfair, God explained His merciful restriction: *"He must not be allowed to reach out his hand and take also from the tree of life and eat, <u>and live forever</u>."* (Genesis 3:22, NIV®) You see, God is merciful - He did not want Adam and Eve to live forever in their sin-prone state.

Heaven, however, is a new and better home with perfected people who will live forever. God will provide a home that corrects all the maladies that afflict us today. Who can fathom a life without death, adventure without pain and suffering, and no more night? It hurts my brain to consider but I enjoy trying.

The last bit about Heaven is going to surprise you. The next chapter reveals why there will be no religion in Heaven.

---

vi GoodReads.com. Retrieved 2/22/2016 at http://www.goodreads.com/quotes/tag/loneliness.

A Home Without Religion

Heaven without religion ... It sounds heretical does it not? One of the common misconceptions about Heaven is that it is one boring church service for eternity. *Religion without end - no thank you!*

HEAVEN

I have good news for your future home.
There is no religion in Heaven. In fact,
when you get to Heaven there will be no
church buildings, no cathedrals, no
mosques, and no temples.[vii] The LORD
Himself is the temple in Heaven because He
will be with us in our future home:

> *God's dwelling place is now among
> the people, and he will dwell with
> them. They will be his people, and
> God himself will be with them and be
> their God. (Revelation 21:22-24,
> NIV®)*

This takes us back to how things were in the
beginning when God created the world. He
would show Himself to Adam and Eve to
take walks with them in the Garden of
Eden.[viii] Heaven will be a place where you
are part of God's family. You will have a

direct and personal relationship with the LORD.

I have more good news for you. Today, there is no religion at all as far as God is concerned.

According to the American Heritage dictionary, religion is:

> *A set of beliefs concerning the cause, nature, and purpose of the universe, especially when considered as the creation of a superhuman agency or agencies, usually involving devotional and ritual observances, and often containing a moral code governing the conduct of human affairs.*[ix]

If you look at this definition carefully it correctly attributes to *religion* the one overarching principle: what you must do to make yourself acceptable to God. Religious observances of various types and degrees. A moral code that says *"You must do this..."* and *"You shall not do that..."*

God has a different plan. He desires a *relationship* not a religion. Jesus' message was not *"Do these things and you can go to Heaven."* Rather, He said, *"Come to me, all you who are weary and burdened, and I will give you rest."* (Matthew 11:28, NIV®) Jesus proclaimed that *He* was the way to Heaven,[x] not a system of good works or rituals.

Think about it. If good works were necessary to put you in a right relationship with God, just how many good works would it require - hundreds, thousands, millions? And what about the quality of those good works - would the benefit to other people be measured in some way? What if you did a million good works that benefited millions of people - could you relax at that point and just coast until you got to Heaven?

God is good - too good to let people wallow in doubt over their relationship with Him. If good works were necessary, you could never be sure your motivation, purpose, and execution were good enough.

Jesus even had some rather harsh words for those who try the path of good works to get to Heaven:

> *Not everyone who says to me, 'Lord, Lord,' will enter the kingdom of heaven, but only the one who does the will of my Father who is in heaven. Many will say to me on that day, 'Lord, Lord, did we not prophesy in your name and in your name drive out demons and in your name perform many miracles?'*

> *Then I will tell them plainly, 'I never knew you. Away from me, you evildoers!' (Matthew 7:21-23, NIV®)*

Whoa! Miracle workers who can preach and drive out demons are not good enough for Heaven so what chance does the average person have?

Fortunately the LORD Jesus *desires* a relationship with you. After all, He is perfect - holy, righteous, loving, gentle, all-powerful, all-knowing. Name one thing an imperfect human being could do that would ever be good enough for God? In truth, no human can do anything that our Creator God can't do - and do it with perfection.

Most human religions use a system of good works or rituals because it seems to resonant with a certain pride we have in ourselves. We want to pull ourselves up by our own bootstraps, to do it ourselves rather than be dependent on anyone else. The thought that there is nothing you can do for God to make Him accept you into Heaven is a stumbling block to many people.

So here is how Jesus approached the question of good works when He was asked about it:

> *Then they asked him, "What must we do to do the works God requires?" Jesus answered, "The work of God is this: to believe in the one he has sent." (John 6:28-29, NIV®)*

Belief is another word for faith. There either a relationship with the LORD (by faith) or a religion (by good works). Jesus explains that Heaven has no religion and He wants nothing to do with it. Stop striving to make God accept you and just believe.

Your journey home is not only possible but certain if you start the journey by faith. You have made it this far in the journey so keep reading to learn about that first step toward Heaven.

[vii] As the Apostle John writes of the revelation of Heaven from Jesus Christ: I did not see a temple in the city, because the Lord God Almighty and the Lamb are its temple. 23 The city does not need the sun or the moon to shine on it, for the glory of God gives it light, and the Lamb is its lamp. 24 The nations will walk by its light, and the kings of the earth will bring their splendor into it. (Revelation 21:22-24, NIV®)

[viii] While God is invisible (Romans 1:20; Colossians 1:15; 1 Timothy 1:17), He sometimes makes His presence known to people in various forms. The beautiful relationship He had with Adam and Eve in the Garden of Eden before their fall into sin is highlighted in Genesis 3:8 where they recognized the sound of Him walking in the garden - clearly God made this a frequent event in the beginning. God finally made His presence known when He became a man - a perfect man born of a virgin. His name was Jesus.

[ix] Dictionary.com. The American Heritage® Idioms Dictionary. Copyright © 2002, 2001, 1995 by Houghton Mifflin Company. Published by Houghton Mifflin Company. Retrieved 2/22/2016 at http://dictionary.reference.com/browse/religion?s=t.

[x] Jesus answered, "I am the way and the truth and the life. No one comes to the Father except through me." (John 14:6, NIV®)

Your Journey Home

By this time you should have a critical concern - how can I be certain I will go to Heaven when I die? Everyone wrestles with this question at some point. The answer will define the level of peace and contentment you have in your life today.

As you read in the last chapter, Jesus wants a relationship not a religion. Here is why:

It is far easier to bend a rule and rationalize the behavior than it is to disappoint a person.

When you are in the presence of a truly good person, do have the urge to curse at them? Do you feel it necessary to punch them in the face? Do you long to steal from them? Of course not ... A truly good person in your presence engenders a certain respect and reverence.

Jesus wants to have a personal relationship with you. Jesus, God in the flesh and LORD of all, is the only One of whom you can rightly say is truly good. He is good far beyond what our finite minds can conceive.

So you have to wonder at this point. *If I am not perfect, then how can I even be in the presence of Jesus?* This is the crux of everyone's dilemma. God is good - perfectly righteous - and you are not. Your imperfections get in the way of that personal relationship. You and me and everyone else in this world fall short of God's righteousness.[xi] The self-willed life is what gets all of us into trouble.

Jesus gave up His perfect life for you so your imperfect life could be forgiven and cleansed. Jesus *"suffered once for sins, the righteous for the unrighteous, to bring you to God."* (1 Peter 3:18, NIV®) He died on a cross for you so you could be forgiven and made righteous in His sight. How incredible is that?

Just to make sure you did not miss the significance of what He did on the cross, Jesus rose from the grave on the third day, never to die again. He wanted you to be certain of your forgiveness and eternal home in Heaven. He also wanted you to realize that He is LORD of all.

Will you trust what the LORD Jesus did for you? It is a matter of faith. Not a blind faith for Jesus was a fact in history. Faith is believing God and doing what He says. Here is how Jesus framed it:

> *The kingdom of God has come near. Repent and believe the good news! (Mark 1:15, NIV®)*

Repentance is a change of heart toward the LORD Jesus *(not good works, remember, but changing your mind about yourself in relation to God)*. Believe the good news that Jesus loves you and wants you to have a personal relationship with Him. Jesus wants you with Him in the wonderful place He is building for you called Heaven.

Is it that simple? For you, it is both profound and simple. A profound life-change from self-willed to God-willed. Yet a simple first step - to choose to believe. For God it is incredibly complex and heart-wrenching. But He did the heart-wrenching part for you because of His great love and mercy.[xii] And so this personal relationship with the LORD Jesus and Heaven itself is a gift from God.[xiii]

No longer be afraid or indifferent. The stakes of eternity and Heaven are just too great. *"Believe in the Lord Jesus, and you will be saved."* (Acts 16:31, NIV®) If you want to explore further this wonderful gift of a personal relationship with God, look in the appendix for a journey through the **GRACE outline** in the **Resources** section.

God's gracious gift of forgiveness and Heaven is both possible and certain for all who believe. Walk with the LORD Jesus on this journey of faith and you will never be alone, lost, or abandoned. No matter what happens on Earth, Jesus said, *"And surely I am with you always, to the very end of the age."* (Matthew 28:20, NIV®) At the end of this age, your amazing journey home will surely end in Heaven.

xi There is no difference between Jew and Gentile, for all have sinned and fall short of the glory of God. (Romans 3:23, NIV®)

xii But because of his great love for us, God, who is rich in mercy, 5 made us alive with Christ even when we were dead in transgressions—it is by grace you have been saved ... For it is by grace you have been saved, through faith—and this is not from yourselves, it is the gift of God— 9 not by works, so that no one can boast. (Ephesians 2:4-5, 8-9, NIV®)

xiii For the wages of sin is death, but the gift of God is eternal life in Christ Jesus our Lord. (Romans 6:23, NIV®)

Starting Your Journey

Your journey home to Heaven starts the moment you choose to believe the good news that Jesus is LORD. He loved you enough to offer His perfect life to pay the penalty for your self-willed life. Then Jesus rose from the dead so you would know that He is everything He claimed to be and accomplished His mission of redemption. Trusting in Him means you are forgiven and given eternal life – a forever love relationship with the LORD Jesus in time and for eternity.

Eternal life is not for the hereafter but in the here and now. Your journey does not wait for your passing but starts today.

> *Now is the time of God's favor, now is the day of salvation. (2 Corinthians 6:2, NIV®)*

So how do you begin the journey home with a God you cannot see? There is a guide book to the journey called the Bible.

Consult the Guide Book

God did not want you to be ignorant of Him or His ways. He provided His inspired word in a collection of 66 books known as *The Bible*. Many people think of the Bible as one book – in that sense it is the best-selling book of all time. The significance of the 66 books is that they were written over roughly a 1,600 year period by some 40 different people. The style of each writer was unique. But long before computers and copiers and the internet, these 40 different people all wrote consistently about the same God with the same characteristics and values. Such an accomplishment in and of itself is nothing short of miraculous.

Neither did God want His word to be lost over the eons of time. He worked to preserve the biblical texts. If you look at other works of antiquity – such as the common literature assignment for high-schoolers, Homer's *The Iliad* and *The Odyssey* – you find that all the copies of ancient manuscripts have many differences in the story content as well as typographical errors. The error rate for these books is up to 25% - a quarter of the book cannot be trusted to be the real story written by Homer.

The Bible manuscripts, on the other hand, are without equal among ancient documents. There is less than one tenth of one percent transmission error in the copies of biblical texts – typographical and transpositional errors, none of which change the primary meaning of the text. The Bible text we read today is a reliable version of what was originally written by the 40 writers – prophets and apostles of long ago.

In the Bible we find everything we need to live the kind of life God desires:

> *His divine power has given us everything we need for a godly life through our <u>knowledge of him</u> who called us by his own glory and goodness. Through these he has given us <u>his very great and precious promises</u>. (2 Peter 1:3-4, NIV®)*

There are also over 7,000 promises in the Bible. While some of these were made for specific situations or people groups, you can be comforted in knowing there are still thousands of promises God made just for you.

A Readable Guide Book

If you already have a Bible, that is terrific. Make sure it is a Bible version that is easy to read. Each version of the Bible is an attempt to translate the original language into modern English in a way that communicates well to the reader. You can explore various versions at a wonderful site called BibleGateway.com. It is free and easy to use for reading and searching through the Bible.

30-Days to Start Your Journey

To jump-start your journey, the following pages provide a daily Bible reading for the next 30 days. There is a small portion of the Bible and some key thoughts to help you understand and apply what you have learned.

Here's the key to reading the Bible – read each verse as though it is a love letter from your loved one who is far away but coming home soon. The Bible was written down for you – treat it as the most important words you will hear today. Then do what He says to do. It is that simple and astonishingly life-changing.

HEAVEN

Day 1

Follow Me

[18] As Jesus was walking beside the Sea of Galilee, he saw two brothers, Simon called Peter and his brother Andrew. They were casting a net into the lake, for they were fishermen. [19] "Come, follow me," Jesus said, "and I will send you out to fish for people." [20] At once they left their nets and followed him. (Matthew 4:18-20, NIV®)

You have to love the simplicity of Jesus - He said to two brothers, *"Come, follow Me."* Do you have difficulties in following others, wanting to chart your own course through life? The self-willed life is one chosen by many. When you look around the world, do you see it constantly trending up or down in terms of goodness, compassion, virtue? Peter, Andrew, James and John deemed following Jesus to be more important than anything else in their lives.

One of our deepest needs is to follow Jesus. Lives are torn apart by the self-willed life to the point that people feel there is no hope. God's will is not for you to follow your own course *(atheism)* or a set of pre-defined rules *(religion)* but simply to journey with Jesus.

Day 2

Follow Who?

¹ In the beginning was the Word, and the Word was with God, and the Word was God. ² He was with God in the beginning. ³ Through him all things were made; without him nothing was made that has been made. ⁴ In him was life, and that life was the light of all mankind. (John 1:1-4, NIV®)

Jesus is referred to here as the *"Word"* - which translates the Greek word *logos*, meaning the full revelation about God. So calling Him *logos* means that we see in Jesus everything we can ever know about God. And the end of verse one makes this clear - *"the Word was God."*

♦ If *"in the beginning"* Jesus already *"was,"* then how long has Jesus been around?
♦ Where was He (v. 2)?
♦ What has He done (v.3)?
♦ What does He possess that each of us needs (v.4)?

Our finite minds cannot comprehend an eternal God – one without beginning or end. Fortunately He does not expect us to figure it all out. We only need to accept and believe what God has chosen to reveal about Himself.

Day 3

Grace and Truth

14 The Word became flesh and made his dwelling among us. We have seen his glory, the glory of the one and only Son, who came from the Father, full of grace and truth … 16 Out of his fullness we have all received grace in place of grace already given. 17 For the law was given through Moses; grace and truth came through Jesus Christ. 18 No one has ever seen God, but the one and only Son, who is himself God and is in closest relationship with the Father, has made him known. (John 1:14,16-18, NIV®)

The glory of God is too bright and awesome for any person to see and live, as God told Moses (Exodus 33:20). How then can we follow the heavenly light of Jesus without being blinded? He came to us veiled in human flesh. He took upon Himself a human nature *("became flesh")* without losing one ounce of His divine nature *("full of grace and truth")* so that you and I could see His glory and follow Him. Jesus revealed grace and truth. Judgment is getting what you deserve. Mercy is not getting what you deserve. But grace is getting what you do not deserve – forgiveness and eternal life. Thank God for giving us grace.

HEAVEN

Day 4

Facets of Grace

8 For it is by grace you have been saved, through faith—and this is not from yourselves, it is the gift of God— 9 not by works, so that no one can boast. 10 For we are God's handiwork, created in Christ Jesus to do good works, which God prepared in advance for us to do. (Ephesians 2:8-10, NIV®)

Like a beautiful gemstone cut and polished for maximum sparkle, grace also shines with many wonderful facets. One facet is the gift of forgiveness – saving us from the pain of a self-willed life. God's grace is offered to everyone. It is received through faith in the LORD Jesus. One cannot do good works to earn God's forgiveness – it is available only through faith.

The second facet of God's grace is its purpose. God wants to create in us something brand new and beautiful. We become God's *"handiwork"* – His mosaic or masterpiece. What does God use to create this beautiful masterpiece in you? A series of good works He planned in advance. While you are not saved *by* good works, you are saved *for* good works. As you cooperate with His plan for your life, He cuts and polishes from the inside-out to reflect His glory on Earth.

Day 5
The Best is Yet to Come

⁷ Jesus said to the servants, "Fill the jars with water"; so they filled them to the brim. ⁸ Then he told them, "Now draw some out and take it to the master of the banquet." They did so, ⁹ and the master of the banquet tasted the water that had been turned into wine. He did not realize where it had come from, though the servants who had drawn the water knew. Then he called the bridegroom aside ¹⁰ and said, "Everyone brings out the choice wine first and then the cheaper wine after the guests have had too much to drink; but you have saved the best till now." (John 2:7-10, NIV®)

As the Creator of all things (John 1:3; Col. 1:15-16), Jesus should not surprise you when He performs miracles – but He always does. At this wedding, they ran out of wine – a big deal in that time. So he turns water into wine. Every miracle had a purpose. Jesus made a point here that He provides only the best. He always has what is best planned for you. It may or may not be via a miracle but you can trust His heart. His best for you is yet to come!

Day 6

A Defining Moment

17 Therefore, if anyone is in Christ, the new creation has come: The old has gone, the new is here! (2 Corinthians 5:17, NIV®)

When you choose to believe in the LORD Jesus as the One who died to set you free from your old self-willed life, you become a *"new creation."* A multitude of things about you change – though you may not feel very different and, frankly, you may not act very different at first. God works from the inside-out as you seek to follow Him. The Bible reveals that God:

- ◆ Chooses to make you holy and blameless in His sight (Ephesians 1:4).
- ◆ Pours out His love into our hearts (Romans 5:5).
- ◆ Begins to work all things out for your good – that you will become more like Jesus (Romans 8:28-29).

Give the LORD praise for the marvelous work He has started in you. Be confident in this: *"that he who began a good work in you will carry it on to completion until the day of Christ Jesus." (Philippians 1:6, NIV®)*

Day 7

A Teachable Moment

⁴ Show me your ways, Lord, teach me your paths. ⁵ Guide me in your truth and teach me, for you are God my Savior, and my hope is in you all day long. ⁶ Remember, Lord, your great mercy and love, for they are from of old· ⁷ Do not remember the sins of my youth and my rebellious ways; according to your love remember me, for you, Lord, are good. (Psalm 25:4-7, NIV®)

God does not want you to wander around in ignorance. He wants you to know and follow His ways. The flip-side is our willingness to follow Him.

♦ Are you teachable and willing to follow Him or...

♦ Will you resume a purposeless, self-willed life?

There are times we all stumble in our journey with the LORD Jesus. Remember these three aspects of God's nature: *mercy, love,* and *goodness.* Our relationship with Him could not survive otherwise. Thank Him for His forgiving nature and gift of eternal life in Heaven. Seek His guidance and trust Him to lead.

Day 8

A Refining Moment

8 If we claim to be without sin, we deceive ourselves and the truth is not in us. 9 If we confess our sins, he is faithful and just and will forgive us our sins and purify us from all unrighteousness (1 John 1:8-9, NIV®)

In any journey, it is inevitable that you will stray from the path. Some think that becoming a Christian means you become perfect in all your ways. Granted, some Christians think they are perfect but their loved ones know better. When you run off-course in following Christ, you do not lose your place in Heaven but hinder the friendship you have with God.

The word *"confess"* means to agree with God that what you did was wrong. You look at it from God's perspective. You can't make up for it. Jesus already paid the price for *all* sins for *all* mankind for *all* time (1 Peter 3:18). You simply offer your confession to God in humility and trust in His grace. Then God forgives, cleanses, and restores your fellowship with Him. In your journey, be sure to keep short accounts in your relationship with God. Stay close to Him so you can follow His lead.

Day 9

When You Call Me

5 "And when you pray, do not be like the hypocrites, for they love to pray standing in the synagogues and on the street corners to be seen by others. Truly I tell you, they have received their reward in full. 6 But when you pray, go into your room, close the door and pray to your Father, who is unseen. Then your Father, who sees what is done in secret, will reward you. 8 ... for your Father knows what you need before you ask him. (Matthew 6:5-6,8, NIV®)

Prayer is your cell phone to God. And, like your mother, God wants to hear from you often – *"when you pray."* Prayer is a life-long conversation where you open up everything in your life to God – your deepest yearnings, the roller-coaster of feelings, the joys and the hurts. God knows everything already (Psalm 33:13-15, 139:1-4; Matthew 9:4, 11:27; John 16:30) so there is no sense in hiding anything from Him. And He made you so He knows everything about you – including all the things that tempt you to stray from His path. Seek His comfort, His guidance, His understanding. Ask for His wisdom and the courage to follow Him. And be sure to spend time in His presence listening.

Day 10

What to Pray

¹ One day Jesus was praying ... one of his disciples said to him, "Lord, teach us to pray, just as John taught his disciples." ² He said to them, "When you pray, say: "'Father, hallowed be your name, your kingdom come. ³ Give us each day our daily bread. ⁴ Forgive us our sins, for we also forgive everyone who sins against us. And lead us not into temptation."'. (Luke 11:1-4, NIV®)

If God knows everything, why do we need to pray? Prayer helps us to get in alignment with God's plan and allows Him to share our burdens. Jesus taught His disciples about the key concerns we should include in our prayers:

- ◆ Worship - Recognition of God's holiness (v.2).
- ◆ Hope – Longing for His future Heaven (v.2).
- ◆ Provision – Asking Him for your daily needs (v.3)
- ◆ Vertical relationship - with God (v.4)
- ◆ Horizontal relationship - with others (v.4)
- ◆ Guidance – Seeking your next step on God's path (v.4).

Day 11
Who Deserves Your Prayers?

¹ I urge, then, first of all, that petitions, prayers, intercession and thanksgiving be made for all people— ² for kings and all those in authority, that we may live peaceful and quiet lives in all godliness and holiness. ³ This is good, and pleases God our Savior, ⁴ who wants all people to be saved and to come to a knowledge of the truth. ⁵ For there is one God and one mediator between God and mankind, the man Christ Jesus, ⁶ who gave himself as a ransom for all people. (1 Timothy 2:1-6, NIV®)

In the timeless comic strip *Peanuts*, Lucy remarked, *"I don't have any problem loving mankind – it's the people I can't stand."* We can all relate to that sentiment. Some people are just hard to love. Yet the Bible tells us to pray for all people, especially for those in positions of authority. God's desire is that we live *"peaceful and quiet lives in all godliness and holiness."* (v.2) Because so many people live self-willed lives instead of God-willed lives, it is necessary to pray for God's constant intervention. Thankfully, no priest is needed – Jesus is our mediator giving us direct access to God. You can pray anytime in any place for anyone.

HEAVEN

Day 12

Truth Confirmed (part 1)

6 Now some teachers of the law were sitting there, thinking to themselves, 7 "Why does this fellow talk like that? He's blaspheming! Who can forgive sins but God alone?" 8 Immediately Jesus knew in his spirit that this was what they were thinking in their hearts, and he said to them, "Why are you thinking these things? 9 Which is easier: to say to this paralyzed man, 'Your sins are forgiven,' or to say, 'Get up, take your mat and walk'? 10 But I want you to know that the Son of Man has authority on earth to forgive sins." So he said to the man, 11 "I tell you, get up, take your mat and go home." 12 He got up, took his mat and walked out in full view of them all. (Mark 2:6-12, NIV®)

When Jesus spoke, people listened. While the religious leaders felt threatened and mocked Jesus, they could not refute the miracles He performed. Jesus did amazing signs such as this healing in full view of the religious leaders and the people in this city. They knew the cripple could not walk before Jesus healed him. Jesus performed these signs so everyone would know they could fully trust what He taught.

Day 13
Truth Confirmed (part 2)

[21] *... Jesus went into the synagogue and began to teach.* [22] *The people were amazed at his teaching, because he taught them as one who had authority ...* [23] *Just then a man in their synagogue who was possessed by an impure spirit cried out,* [24] *"What do you want with us, Jesus of Nazareth? Have you come to destroy us? I know who you are—the Holy One of God!"* [25] *"Be quiet!" said Jesus sternly. "Come out of him!"* [26] *The impure spirit ... came out of him with a shriek.* [27] *The people were all so amazed that they asked each other, "What is this? A new teaching—and with authority! (Mark 1:21-27, NIV®)*

In the 1st century, religious teaching depended on what previous teachers said was true. Jesus taught people the word of God without relying on the often conflicting interpretations of human teachers. But Jesus wanted them to be sure – so He provided miraculous signs. Miracles were not for puffing up His public profile. Jesus only wants you accept and believe God's word. Healing the sick, casting out demons, and raising the dead are clear signs that God is at work and His word is true.

HEAVEN

Day 14

The Most Important Thing

> *35 One of them, an expert in the law, tested him with this question: 36 "Teacher, which is the greatest commandment in the Law?" 37 Jesus replied: "'Love the Lord your God with all your heart and with all your soul and with all your mind.' 38 This is the first and greatest commandment. 39 And the second is like it: 'Love your neighbor as yourself.' 40 All the Law and the Prophets hang on these two commandments."*
> *(Matthew 22:35-40, NIV®)*

God's word has many commands, principles, and instruction on how to live well in God's creation. No one is better suited to tell us how to live than the One who created it all. But what is the most important thing we should do? One of the religious leaders asked Jesus this very question. The most important commandment is actually two intertwined: *Love God* with everything you have and *love others* in the same way. You cannot truly love God without loving the people He made. And you cannot know how to love people without loving God and receiving His love for you. Everything in life starts and ends with this priority.

Day 15

The Capacity to Love

16 For God so loved the world that he gave his one and only Son [Jesus], that whoever believes in him shall not perish but have eternal life. 17 For God did not send his Son into the world to condemn the world, but to save the world through him. 18 Whoever believes in him is not condemned... (John 3:16-18, NIV®)

What would it take for you to be able to love that family member who was so cruel to you growing up? How can you ever love someone who has betrayed you? While these situations seem impossible to us, God sees them differently. You see *"God created mankind in his own image" (Genesis 1:27, NIV®) "In his own image"* means that every human being is worthy of basic respect and civility. Moreover, though sin separates us from God, He chose not to condemn but to act redemptively because of His great love. Jesus gave up His perfect life so you could have eternal life. There is no greater love than One who would give His own life for you. His plan today is not one of condemnation but redemption. Since you are loved without limit, you can love others in the same way. Draw from His limitless well and learn to truly love.

Day 16

More Than Just Bread

35 Then Jesus declared, "I am the bread of life. Whoever comes to me will never go hungry, and whoever believes in me will never be thirsty ... 39 And this is the will of him who sent me, that I shall lose none of all those he has given me, but raise them up at the last day. (John 6:35,39, NIV®)

You have security in knowing that the LORD Jesus holds your life and fate in His hands. He has promised to provide for all your needs: *"31 So do not worry, saying, 'What shall we eat?' or 'What shall we drink?' or 'What shall we wear?' 32 For the pagans run after all these things, and your heavenly Father knows that you need them. 33 But seek first his kingdom and his righteousness, and all these things will be given to you as well." (Matthew 6:31-33, NIV®)*

Even in physical death, the LORD will provide for your needs. The body may die but your soul/spirit is eternal. Jesus will one day raise your physical body and reunite it with your spirit. The resurrection body will last forever in God's perfect home called Heaven. This is your great hope. Trust and believe in Jesus as the *"bread of life"* – your perfect provision.

Day 17

Mountain Moving Faith

37 A furious squall came up, and the waves broke over the boat, so that it was nearly swamped. 38 Jesus was in the stern, sleeping on a cushion. The disciples woke him and said to him, "Teacher, don't you care if we drown?" 39 He got up, rebuked the wind and said to the waves, "Quiet! Be still!" Then the wind died down and it was completely calm. 40 He said to his disciples, "Why are you so afraid? Do you still have no faith?" (Mark 4:37-40, NIV®)

Faith is believing God and doing what He says. The issue is not how much faith you have – as if you could manufacture something within yourself to change anything in God's creation. What makes a difference is having the LORD Jesus as the object of your faith. I could call my kitchen table *"God"* but all my prayers would be worthless. The object of my faith would be a stick of wood. If, however, your faith is in the Creator of all things: *"... Truly I tell you, if you have faith as small as a mustard seed, you can say to this mountain, 'Move from here to there,' and it will move. Nothing will be impossible for you.'" (Matthew 17:20, NIV®)*

Day 18

Practical Faith

14 They came to him [Jesus] and said, "Teacher, we know that you are a man of integrity. You aren't swayed by others, because you pay no attention to who they are; but you teach the way of God in accordance with the truth. Is it right to pay the imperial tax to Caesar or not? 15 Should we pay or shouldn't we?" But Jesus knew their hypocrisy. "Why are you trying to trap me?" he asked. "Bring me a denarius and let me look at it." 16 They brought the coin, and he asked them, "Whose image is this? And whose inscription?" "Caesar's," they replied. 17 Then Jesus said to them, "Give back to Caesar what is Caesar's and to God what is God's." And they were amazed at him. (Mark 12:14-17, NIV®)

If you follow Christ, how can you live in a world of self-willed people, corrupt governments, and morally ambiguous employers? The world is complicated by sin. Yet Jesus showed us that we are to live in the world and shine the light of His truth. Give the government and your employer what you rightfully owe them. As you go through life, share the love and message of Christ to shine a bright light in a dark world.

Day 19

Remember the Cross

23 For I received from the Lord what I also passed on to you: The Lord Jesus, on the night he was betrayed, took bread, 24 and when he had given thanks, he broke it and said, "This is my body, which is for you; do this in remembrance of me." 25 In the same way, after supper he took the cup, saying, "This cup is the new covenant in my blood; do this, whenever you drink it, in remembrance of me." 26 For whenever you eat this bread and drink this cup, you proclaim the Lord's death until he comes. (1 Corinthians 11:23-26, NIV®)

Communion or the LORD's Supper is practiced by the church congregation prayerfully taking a bite of unleavened bread and a sip of wine (or grape juice). The bread represents the body of Christ nailed to the cross. The wine represents His blood shed for your redemption (Ephesians 1:7).

A simple reading of the Bible here indicates the LORD's Supper is a reminder to all of the death of Christ on the cross for the sins of the whole world. It is a memorial lest anyone would ever forget the enormous cost to grant you Heaven.

HEAVEN

Day 20

The First Easter

¹ On the first day of the week, very early in the morning, the women took the spices they had prepared and went to the tomb. ² They found the stone rolled away from the tomb, ³ but when they entered, they did not find the body of the Lord Jesus. ⁴ ... suddenly two men in clothes that gleamed like lightning stood beside them. ⁵ ... the men said to them, "Why do you look for the living among the dead? ⁶ He is not here; he has risen! Remember how he told you, while he was still with you in Galilee: ⁷ 'The Son of Man must be delivered over to the hands of sinners, be crucified and on the third day be raised again.'" (Luke 24:1-7, NIV®)

Easter is a traditional holiday that reminds us that Jesus rose from the grave, proving He is LORD and that His sacrifice for sin was accepted. He predicted His death and resurrection (Matthew 20:18-20, 26:1-2,32; Mark 8:31, 9:9,31, 10:33-34; Luke 18:32-34). Here we see the culmination of His earthly ministry. By Jesus' resurrection power, He can and will grant eternal life to all who call on His name. He is not dead – He has risen!

Day 21

Trouble With a Capital T

I have told you these things, so that in me you may have peace. In this world you will have trouble. But take heart! I have overcome the world. (John 16:33, NIV®)

Out of thousands of promises in the Bible, this one stands out as *bad news/ good news*. The bad news is that trouble is part of life on Planet Earth. Becoming a Christian does not change this fact. The good news is that Jesus says *"take heart"* – do not be afraid of what is happening or may happen in the future. The LORD Jesus has it under control. After all, He has overcome death itself – so what trouble can come your way that Jesus cannot handle?

Note that Jesus did not say you have to handle troubles by yourself. He has overcome the world. As a follower of Jesus, you have His promise that *"in Me"* you will have peace in the midst of any storm. And just before He ascended to Heaven, He told us, *"surely I am with you always, to the very end of the age." (Matthew 28:20, NIV®)*

Just how big is your trouble? May I say that the LORD Jesus is far greater. Let not your heart be troubled!

HEAVEN

Day 22

What Were You Thinking?

8 Finally, brothers and sisters, whatever is true, whatever is noble, whatever is right, whatever is pure, whatever is lovely, whatever is admirable—if anything is excellent or praiseworthy—think about such things. 9 Whatever you have learned or received or heard from me, or seen in me—put it into practice. And the God of peace will be with you. (Philippians 4:8-9, NIV®)

He was a young consultant with an impossible assignment. Everything that could go wrong began playing over and over in his head. He questioned his abilities. His boss must not like him. Fear turned into anger as he dwelled on the seeming unjust treatment. Continuing through the night without sleep, the young man finally penned a resignation letter – he couldn't take it anymore.

What we think and how we think drive how we live. Train yourself to think about things that are true *(reality-based)*, noble, righteous, and excellent. As you study the Bible, dwell on a verse that stands out to you. God will grant you peace inside as your thoughts and actions align with what He has declared to be true.

Day 23

Change is a Process

²² You were taught, with regard to your former way of life, to put off your old self, which is being corrupted by its deceitful desires; ²³ to be made new in the attitude of your minds; ²⁴ and to put on the new self, created to be like God in true righteousness and holiness. (Ephesians 4:22-24, NIV®)

When is a thief not a thief? The answer is simple: when he becomes something else. Simply putting a thief behind bars does not make the thief something else – you just prevent him from stealing. The thief must turn his selfishness into generosity through honest work so he can share with others.

While you may not be a thief, your Christian life is all about change – becoming more like Jesus in your journey. There is a *"former way of life"* – before you put your faith in the LORD Jesus – that you must make a conscious choice to *"put off."* You *"put on"* the new life – walking with Jesus – as another conscious choice. You also work on your *"attitude"* – renewing your mind as you seek to understand God's will and His ways. You were created for *"righteousness."* Change is a process - take it one day at a time.

Day 24

People Are Not Your Enemy

10 Finally, be strong in the Lord and in his mighty power. 11 Put on the full armor of God, so that you can take your stand against the devil's schemes. 12 For our struggle is not against flesh and blood, but against the rulers, against the authorities, against the powers of this dark world and against the spiritual forces of evil in the heavenly realms. (Ephesians6:10-12, NIV®)

Following Jesus makes you a target for criticism and false accusations. When conflict arises, you have a critical choice. You can choose to make that person your enemy or you can look at the situation from God's point of view. Each person is made in the image of God. Our *"struggle is not against flesh and blood"* – meaning people. We do not fight *against* people but we fight *for* truth. We have a three-fold enemy: our own self-willed nature, a world system opposed to what God says is righteous, and the devil – a fallen angel bent on destroying God's work and His people. It can be a cruel world so draw your strength from the LORD Jesus and seek His protection from evil. Then you can keep loving people as Jesus loves you.

Day 25

Forgiveness, Forgiveness, Forgiveness

[3] "If your brother or sister sins against you, rebuke them; and if they repent, forgive them. [4] Even if they sin against you seven times in a day and seven times come back to you saying 'I repent,' you must forgive them." [5] The apostles said to the Lord, "Increase our faith!" (Luke 17:3-5, NIV®)

All of us will be hurt by someone at some point. Some people offend or betray or lie or cheat us more than once. How can you forgive someone once, much less over and over again?

Jesus taught His disciples to work through the process of forgiveness. When someone offends you, go to them privately and let them know what happened. *"If they repent"* you are to forgive them –even if it happens multiple times. Jesus was not setting a limit of seven times to forgive someone. Rather He was making the point that you freely offer forgiveness.

The disciples asked for more faith – the task seemed impossible. Consider that Jesus gave His life for ALL your sins. Is it too hard for you to forgive someone one time? What about two times? Even seventy times seven?

Day 26

Love in Action

16 This is how we know what love is: Jesus Christ laid down his life for us. And we ought to lay down our lives for our brothers and sisters. 17 If anyone has material possessions and sees a brother or sister in need but has no pity on them, how can the love of God be in that person? 18 Dear children, let us not love with words or speech but with actions and in truth. (1 John 3:16-18, NIV®)

The love defined here is an action: *A decision of the will carried into action that meets the needs of another without any expectation of a reward.* God loved us by acting redemptively. So as one redeemed by the LORD, how should you respond? Act redemptively toward others. *"And we ought to lay down our lives for our brothers and sisters."* This is the *Semper Fi* mentality of a marine -- always faithful! But if you refuse to meet the needs of others, even though you could act on it...*"how can the love of God be in [you]?"* Saying *I'll pray for you* is a nice sentiment but of little help for one who is hungry – take them food. Be alert as needs arise in your life zones. Do what you can when you can. Love is an action verb.

Day 27

Bearing Fruit

²² But the fruit of the Spirit is love, joy, peace, forbearance, kindness, goodness, faithfulness, ²³ gentleness and self-control. Against such things there is no law. ²⁴ Those who belong to Christ Jesus have crucified the flesh with its passions and desires. ²⁵ Since we live by the Spirit, let us keep in step with the Spirit. (Galatians 5:22-25, NIV®)

Did you ever see a tree suddenly display fruit on its branches? Of course not. A tree bears fruit gradually. It needs water, sunshine, good soil for nourishment, and time. This is also true of the Christian life as well – God does not instantaneously change you but works to bears fruit in your life over time.

Your new life in Christ will blossom into:
- ♦ Inner qualities of *love, joy, peace*
- ♦ Relational qualities of *patience, kindness, goodness*
- ♦ Discipline qualities of *faithfulness, gentleness, self-control*

If you feel like you fall short in any of these areas, ask the LORD for His help. He will never make you feel foolish for asking.

Day 28

Power to Be a Witness

> *6 ..."Lord, are you at this time going to restore the kingdom to Israel?" 7 He said to them: "It is not for you to know the times or dates the Father has set by his own authority. 8 But you will receive power when the Holy Spirit comes on you; and you will be my witnesses in Jerusalem, and in all Judea and Samaria, and to the ends of the earth." (Acts 1:6-8, NIV®)*

Jesus stayed with His disciples for 40 days after His resurrection offering many convincing proofs that it truly was Himself risen from the dead. His disciples asked about the predicted kingdom of God centered in Israel – literally Heaven on Earth. Would He make that happen right away? But that was not the top priority for Jesus. He called His followers to be His witnesses on Earth. Jesus did not call for perfection, nor to sit on a mountain and pretend to be a holy man, nor to become Mother Teresa. He promised God the Holy Spirit would come upon you to empower you as His witness. The Holy Spirit dwells within you the moment you trust in the LORD Jesus. Follow Jesus. Share His love and message with others. You have the power according to His promise.

Day 29

Unashamed

¹⁶ *For I am not ashamed of the gospel, because it is the power of God that brings salvation to everyone who believes: first to the Jew, then to the Gentile.* ¹⁷ *For in the gospel the righteousness of God is revealed—a righteousness that is by faith from first to last. (Romans 1:16-17, NIV®)*

"Pride goes before destruction" (Proverbs 16:18, NIV®) says the proverb. But there is a good kind of pride: the pride you have in parents who raised you well while sacrificing for your future, the pride you have in your child who sees someone in need and wants to help, the pride you have in a job well done.

What kind of pride should you have for the LORD Jesus who gave His life for you? The kind of pride that upholds His good name and reputation in a world that often uses *Jesus* as no more than a curse word. As one who has been redeemed, you should be unashamed of Jesus and your faith in Him. Does this mean you go around bashing people that are different from you? No, no, no! Our job is to love people without condition and to be *"testifying to the good news of God's grace." (Acts 20:24, NIV®)*

HEAVEN

Day 30

Soon!

12 "Look, I am coming soon! My reward is with me, and I will give to each person according to what they have done. 13 I am the Alpha and the Omega, the First and the Last, the Beginning and the End. (Revelation 22:12-13, NIV®)

Jesus spoke these words in the last chapter of the last book in the Bible, the book of Revelation. The word *"soon"* means imminent – His return could happen at any time. Though we do not know the date and time of Jesus' return, we do know we are some 2,000 years closer to *"soon."*

Will you be ready? Will you be looking forward to seeing Jesus face-to-face? *"28 And now, dear children, continue in him, so that when he appears we may be confident and unashamed before him at his coming. 29 If you know that he is righteous, you know that everyone who does what is right has been born of him." (1 John 2:28-29, NIV®)* Keep seeking and following the LORD Jesus. Be alert to anyone and anything that would diminish your love for Jesus: *"Therefore keep watch, because you do not know on what day your Lord will come." (Matthew 24:42, NIV®)*

Resources

Topic	Summary
The GRACE Outline	*Five powerful points to help you understand God's grace that provides you can with an eternal relationship of love with the LORD Jesus.*
You Can Trust What Jesus Says	*Jesus said some great things but how can we know He spoke the truth? Can you trust what He said? Find out here.*

The GRACE Outline

Contrary to what you often hear about God from other people, the Bible tells us that God is a God of grace. Grace is a kindness expressed to you even though you do not deserve it. Since God is holy and perfectly righteous, the only way that He could relate to anyone is by grace.

> *For it is by grace you have been saved, through faith – and this not from yourselves, it is the gift of God – not by works, so that no one can boast. (Ephesians 2:8-9, NIV®)*

By grace and not by works, the God who created all things allows you to enter into a relationship with Him forever. Each letter of the word GRACE illustrates a key aspect of the tremendous grace that God extends to you through His Son, Jesus Christ.

HEAVEN

The Good News of God's GRACE is:

♦ **Gracious** - God loves you and everyone else (John 3:16).

♦ **Righteous** - Though God is holy and you are not, He is still willing to give you eternal life (Romans 6:23).

♦ **Acceptance** - Jesus makes you acceptable to God by dying for ALL your sins (1 Peter 3:18).

♦ **Certainty** - Jesus rose from the dead so you can be sure you are forgiven (Romans 4:25).

♦ **Eternal Life** - Eternal life is a forever relationship with God that starts the moment you choose to believe (John 5:24).

G stands for Gracious

Grace point: God loves you and everyone else.

For God so loved the world that He gave His One and Only Son [Jesus], that whoever believes in Him shall not perish but have eternal life. (John 3:16, NIV®)

Is there someone you know that is a really, really, good person? Do you think God loves that person more than you? The reality of God's grace is that He cannot love you any less than the best person you know. He is your Creator and loves you because He gave you life. God is gracious in loving people even though their attitudes and actions sometimes fall short of His righteousness. This reflects His grace extended to you...

R stands for Righteous

Grace point: Though God is righteous and you are not, He is still willing to give you eternal life.

For the wages of sin is death, but the gift of God is eternal life in Christ Jesus our Lord. (Romans 6:23, NIV®)

Could God be truly loving without being righteous as well? Love is founded on righteousness. So God defines the boundaries for our behavior (thoughts, words, deeds) as righteousness. Every human being falls short – the Bible calls this sin. Nevertheless, God is willing to give you eternal life as a reflection of His grace...

A stands for Acceptance

Grace point: Jesus makes you acceptable to God by dying for ALL your sins!

For Christ died for sins once for all, the righteous for the unrighteous, to bring you to God. (1 Peter 3:18, NIV®)

Can God accept you, knowing all that you have said and done in your life? God made the greatest sacrifice for you to make you acceptable. God became a man, Jesus, and lived the perfect life that you and I can never live. Then He offered His perfect life for you on a cross. His sacrifice for your sins brings forgiveness within your grasp. Grace upon grace is offered to you...

C stands for Certainty

Grace point: Jesus rose from the dead so you can be sure you are forgiven!

Jesus was handed over to die for our sins. He was raised to life in order to make us right with God. (Romans 4:25, NIRV)

Can God truly forgive you? Yes, Jesus not only died for you but He rose from the dead so that you can know with certainty that His sacrifice was acceptable, your sins are forgiven, and that you can have a good relationship with God forever. This grace gives you confidence to enter into a relationship with Him...

E stands for Eternal Life

Grace point: Eternal life is a forever relationship with God that starts the moment you choose to believe!

Whoever hears my word and believes him who sent me has eternal life and will not be condemned. (John 5:24, NIV®)

Because of the grace that God has extended to you, you can enjoy a personal relationship with Him forever – this is eternal life. It starts when you stop trying to live life without Him (going your own way) and turn to the LORD Jesus. This is not about rules but relationship. When you follow the LORD Jesus, He will guide you in the path you should go. Will this mean changes? Absolutely! By grace God meets you where you are and will work to transform you daily into the person He wants you to be ...

Now that you have seen and understand God's gift of grace to you, is there any reason you would not want to accept God's grace?

> Yet to all who did receive him, to those who believed in his name, he gave the right to become children of God—children born not of natural descent, nor of human decision or a husband's will, but born of God. (John 1:12-13, NIV®)

Will you prayerfully accept God's grace? You can be forgiven of your sins and enter into a relationship with the LORD Jesus starting right now. Here is a prayer you might pray – the specific words are not a magic formula. God knows your thoughts and considers the sincerity of your words.

Dear LORD Jesus,

Though I am a sinner, You are gracious. Thank you for forgiving my sins and giving me eternal life. I believe in You and will follow you as my LORD and Savior. Amen!

If you meant these words when you prayed to the LORD, He heard your prayer and granted you eternal life. You ARE forgiven, you ARE loved, and you ARE a child of God now. Welcome to God's family!

Be sure to go and tell as many people as you can about the wonderful GRACE that God has bestowed on you.

HEAVEN

The Gospel of GRACE

For it by grace you have been saved, through faith ... (Ephesians 2:8, NIV)

G stands for Gracious

>>> God loves you and everyone else in the world.

For God so loved the world that He gave His One and Only Son that whoever believes in Him should not perish but have eternal life (John 3:16, NIV).

R stands for Righteous

>>> Though God is righteous and you are not,
>>> He is willing to give you eternal life.

The wages of sin is death but the gift of God is eternal life through Christ Jesus our LORD (Romans 6:23, NIV).

A stands for Acceptance

>>> Jesus Christ makes you acceptable to God
>>> by dying for all your sins.

Christ died for sins, once for all, the Righteous for the unrighteous, to bring you to God (1 Peter 3:18, NIV).

C stands for Certainty

>>> Jesus Christ rose from the dead so
>>> you can be sure you are forgiven.

Jesus was handed over to die for our sins. He was raised to life ... to make us right with God. (Romans 4:25, NIrV).

E stands for Eternal Life

>>>Eternal life is a forever relationship with God
>>> that starts the moment you choose to believe.

Jesus said, "Whoever hears My word and believes Him who sent me has eternal life and will not be condemned (John 5:24, NIV).

50-count packs of 3x5 cards (color / black & white) with the GRACE outline are available online at WordTruthPress.com.

You Can Trust What Jesus Says

Jesus made some amazing claims about truth. First He said, *"I am ... The Truth." (John 14:6, NIV®)* Later He explained: *"In fact, the reason I was born and came into the world is to testify to the truth." (John 18:37, NIV®)* If Jesus is the Truth and speaks only what is true, then He is absolutely trustworthy in His teachings. But the question remains - how can we know what Jesus said is true?

Testimony of Friends

First, His friends testified that Jesus was without sin: Peter (Acts 3:14, 7:52; 1 Pet. 3:18), John (1 John 2:1,29), Paul (2 Cor.

5:21), the writer of Hebrews (Heb. 9:14). Of course your friends will always back you up and build you up (otherwise they aren't really your friends, right?). But what about His enemies?

Testimony of Enemies

Even the enemies of Jesus attest to His veracity. The Samaritans were a group that hated the Jews. Yet when Jesus spoke to Samaritans in one city, they believed Him (John 4:39-42) - truly remarkable for people that hated Him for His ethnicity. Roman guards were sent by the religious leaders to arrest Jesus. Returning without Him they exclaimed, *"No one ever spoke the way this man does." (John 7:46, NIV)* The religious leaders assailed the ignorance of the guards, claiming they were deceived - meaning the guards were certain what Jesus said was true. After questioning Jesus, Pontius Pilate, the Governor of Judea who would have Jesus executed, could find nothing false in what Jesus professed. Even the religious leaders of the Sanhedrin who put Jesus on trial could not find one thing false in what Jesus said or did (Matthew 26:57-60).

Miracles to Back Up His Words

When Jesus taught people in groups, He often used miracles to confirm the truth they were hearing (John 5:36). At one point, a paralyzed man was brought to Jesus. Rather than simply heal the man,

Jesus chose to teach the crowd an important truth:

> 5 ...He said to the paralyzed man, "Son, your sins are forgiven." 6 Now some teachers of the law were sitting there, thinking to themselves, 7 "Why does this fellow talk like that? He's blaspheming! Who can forgive sins but God alone?" 8 Immediately Jesus knew in his spirit that this was what they were thinking in their hearts, and he said to them, "Why are you thinking these things? 9 Which is easier: to say to this paralyzed man, 'Your sins are forgiven,' or to say, 'Get up, take your mat and walk'? 10 But <u>I want you to know that the Son of Man has authority</u> on earth to forgive sins." So he said to the man, 11 "I tell you, get up, take your mat and go home." 12 He got up, took his mat and walked out in full view of them all. This amazed everyone and they praised God, saying, "We have never seen anything like this!" (Mark 2:5-12, NIV, emphasis mine)

Healing the sick, opening the eyes and ears of the lame, calming the raging seas, and raising the dead were great miracles performed to confirm to His followers that everything He said was true.

Predicting the Future Successfully

Over and over during His earthly ministry, Jesus predicted the future. Some of the things He predicted would take place many years later. But Jesus also predicted specific events in His own life that His followers could have easily discredited. They could not because the predictions came true before their very eyes. Consider this small set of predictions and fulfillments:

Jesus' Prediction	Foretold	Fulfilled
One of His 12 closest disciples (Judas) would betray Him	Matthew 26:21	Luke 22:47-48
Peter would deny He knew Jesus 3 times in one night	Matt. 26:33-34	Matthew 26:74-75
The religious leaders would crucify Him	Luke 24:7	John 19:14-16
He would rise from the dead on the 3rd Day	Matthew 20:18-19; John 2:18-22	Matthew 16:21

Jesus' Prediction	Foretold	Fulfilled
Jerusalem would be overrun in one generation	Luke 19:43-44, 21:20; Matt. 24:34	Titus, who would later become Emporor of Rome, led the campaign to quash the Jewish rebellion. Jerusalem was retaken in A.D. 70. [1]
The Temple in Jerusalem would be destroyed in one generation	Matt. 24:1-2,34	Historian Josephus provides an eyewitness account of the temple of Herod being destroyed by firein A.D. 70[2] during the campaign of Titus. [3]

The preponderance of testimony about Jesus provides ample reason to trust every word of Jesus. Add to that His miracles and ability to foretell future events in His own life. All of these facts point to the supernatural, divine nature of Jesus. He is trustworthy and His words are true. You can trust what Jesus says as recorded in the Bible.

About the Author

Randy Lariscy has a desire to go to Heaven but realizes that God has him on this planet to accomplish a kingdom mission. Spreading the grace of the LORD Jesus is his primary focus. Randy works as a bivocational minister in both the business and ministry worlds. This gives Randy many unique insights into how people view God and spiritual matters in general.

His spiritual gifts and passion have concentrated his ministry work in discipleship and evangelism. His ministry roles have been varied including that of an Education Pastor, Evangelism Consultant, Radio Bible Teacher, and Supply Preacher. His latest role was with Piedmont Church in Marietta, Georgia working to strengthen their Bible study groups.

He holds a B.B.A. In Finance, M.A. In Pastoral Ministry, Master of Divinity, and Doctorate in Theology. Residing in Marietta, Georgia, Randy is happily married with two adult children and three grandchildren *(so far)*.

Quality resources with significant spiritual impact

On the web at **WordTruthPress.com**

Look for more great resources from WordTruth Press:

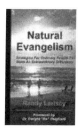

	Natural Evangelism
	Strategies for Ordinary People to Make an Extraordinary Difference
	Evangelism should be as natural as breathing but for many believers it is a word that leaves you breathless. Natural Evangelism is a lifestyle of sharing the love and message of Christ in the context of relationships you form along the way. Discover five long-term strategies that ordinary believers can practice in their everyday life zones. Use these strategies to develop prospects, create natural opportunities to share the good news, and see people develop a personal relationship with the LORD Jesus.

 *Available now* *$9.95 USD*	**Portraits of Forgiveness** *Finding the Inspiration and Courage to Forgive* Like an old, frayed blanket there are many loose threads in our relationships. Issues and conflict divide us from family, friends, and innumerable people we encounter throughout life. The process of forgiveness is necessary to restore and rebuild those relationships. In this book you will find great stories of how God works in the lives of people to bring about forgiveness and reconciliation - binding up the loose threads and making relationships even stronger than before.
 $9.95 USD Qty 50	**The Ten Commandments** *Evangelism Tract (Qty 50)* The Ten Commandments are shown on the front of this 3x5 card with a positive version of each command. On the back is a presentation of the gospel. It is printed with a glossy, color front and black-and-white back.
 $9.95 USD Qty 50	**The Gospel of GRACE** *Evangelism Tract (Qty 50)* This attractive 3x5 card presents the good news using the word GRACE as an acrostic. Each letter represents a different aspect of God's grace at work in salvation. Glossy, color front and black-and-white back.

	Speedy Devotions
	Volume One – Wise Choices
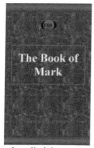 *Available now* *$12.95 USD*	Do you have only a little time to study the Bible? Or does the Bible seem intimidating in its size and scope? Many find it hard to stay focused on long passages of Scripture. Yet the Bible is God's word for all people. And even a small amount of God's word can have a profound impact on your life. Volume 1 is about wise choices. This devotional takes you through the book of Proverbs where you learn great wisdom in small portions each day
	The Book of Mark
	Volume 1: Chapters 1-6
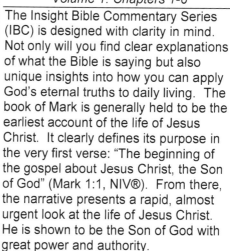 *Available now* *$9.95 USD*	The Insight Bible Commentary Series (IBC) is designed with clarity in mind. Not only will you find clear explanations of what the Bible is saying but also unique insights into how you can apply God's eternal truths to daily living. The book of Mark is generally held to be the earliest account of the life of Jesus Christ. It clearly defines its purpose in the very first verse: "The beginning of the gospel about Jesus Christ, the Son of God" (Mark 1:1, NIV®). From there, the narrative presents a rapid, almost urgent look at the life of Jesus Christ. He is shown to be the Son of God with great power and authority.

The mission of WordTruth Press is to provide quality Bible-based resources with significant spiritual impact for individuals and churches. Education and evangelism are the main focus of WordTruth Press. Following the Great Commission of the LORD Jesus[xiv] this organization provides Bible-based resources to evangelize the world, encourage and equip believers and churches for evangelism, and provide solid Bible teaching to build up the body of Christ.

A key strategy is to find low-cost channels for production and distribution to maximize the availability of our resources to people around the world. WordTruth Press also offers many free resources for churches and individuals available online at: **www.WordTruthPress.com**

[xiv] Matthew 28:18-20.

Made in the USA
Charleston, SC
15 May 2016